Yesterday's Denver

Seemann's Historic Cities Series

No. 1: *Yesterday's Tampa* by Hampton Dunn

No. 2: *Yesterday's Miami* by Nixon Smiley

No. 3: *Yesterday's St. Petersburg* by Hampton Dunn

No. 4: *Yesterday's Key West* by Stan Windhorn & Wright Langley

No. 5: *Yesterday's Sarasota* by Del Marth

No. 6: *Yesterday's Clearwater* by Hampton Dunn

No. 7: *Yesterday's Tallahassee* by Hampton Dunn

No. 8: *Yesterday's Atlanta* by Franklin M. Garrett

No. 9: *Yesterday's Detroit* by Frank Angelo

No. 10: *Yesterday's Denver* by Sandra Dallas

No. 11: *Yesterday's Cape Cod* by Evelyn Lawson (Spring 1975)

No. 12: *Yesterday's Florida Keys* by Stan Windhorn & Wright Langley

Seemann's Historic Cities Series No. 10

Yesterday's
DENVER

by Sandra Dallas

E. A. Seemann Publishing, Inc.
Miami, Florida

Library of Congress Cataloging in Publication Data

Dallas, Sandra
    Yesterday's Denver

    (Seemann's historic cities series no. 10
    1. Denver--Description--Views. 2. Denver--History
--Pictorial works. I. Title.
F784.D4D32   917.88'83'030222   74-81531
ISBN 0-912458-43-7

Copyright © 1974 by Sandra Dallas
Library of Congress Catalog Card No. 74-81531
ISBN 0-912458-43-7

Manufactured in the United States of America

For Dad

Contents

PREFACE   /   9

YESTERDAY'S DENVER   /   11

THE BOOM YEARS (1879-1899)   /   35

SETTLING IN (1900-1920)   /   75

QUEEN CITY OF THE PLAINS (1921-1945)   /   121

Preface

ONLY A FEW MONTHS after Green Russell first sloshed the Cherry Creek waters in his gold pan, Denver activity was avidly recorded by photographers. The first photographic shop was operated at 14th and Larimer in 1859 by George Wakely, who printed "the human face divine" on leather. Other photographers followed, their sensitive, cumbersome equipment piled on ox-carts or stowed on the backs of packhorses. The most famous was William H. Jackson, who photographed Denver from the covered wagon days to the airplane era, and L. C. McClure, a Jackson apprentice who was as intrigued with people as buildings, a rarity among turn-of-the-century photographers.

The photographs of both Jackson and McClure are included here (Wakely's memorable portraiture, alas, has not survived), along with the work of a number of other photographers, many anonymous.

In compiling this work I am indebted to James H. Davis, Opal Harber, Kay Kane, Hazel Lundberg, Augie Mastrogiuseppe, Lynn Taylor, Sandra Turner, and Kay Wilcox, of the Western History Dept., Denver Public Library, and to Maxine Benson and Terry Mangan of the State Historical Society of Colorado. Others who deserve thanks: Caroline Bancroft, Larry Cantwell, Robert Duncan, Dodie Engel, Orville Gleed, William Howland, Beatrice Jordan, R. James Kercheville, Fred Mazzulla, Jean McCormick, Stanton Peckham, Peter R. van Dernoot, Pat Wetzler, Robert Williford, and Mr. and Mrs. Deane Writer.

The following abbreviations are used in picture credits: Western History Dept., Denver Public Library (DPL), State Historical Society of Colorado (SHSC), Lowry Air Force Base (Lowry), Collection of Fred and Jo Mazzulla (Mazzulla). Additional photographs have been furnished by Carolyn

Bancroft, William Howland, First National Bank of Denver, Gates Rubber Co., Mountain Bell, and Samsonite Corp.

SANDRA DALLAS

May 1, 1974

IMPATIENT GOLDSEEKERS without the price of a decent outfit pushed across the prairie with hand-carts to the gold country known as "Pikes Peak." The carts served a dual purpose: prospectors expected to load them with solid gold nuggets to take back home.

Yesterday's Denver

IT WAS 1878, in Leadville, a dreary town that clings tenaciously to the tree-less top of Colorado's mountains, two miles above sea level, under skies that are alternately brittle and cloudless or brooding, leaden with snow. A pair of rancid cobblers, hopelessly inexpert in mining, approached storekeeper H. A. W. Tabor for a grubstake. For Tabor, a luckless prospector himself, grub-staking—proving food and equipment in exchange for a share of improbable wealth—was simply a handout, but he was an easy touch, and he told the shiftless pair to take what they needed. The two prospectors helped them-selves to supplies, and, in a moment of greed, they slipped in a jug of whis-key. It was an auspicious bit of pilfering.

Once out of town, the two unplugged the jug, and partway through, they decided, since they knew little about mining anyway, they might just as well dig where they were. A few yards in either direction they would have missed it, but straight down, 25 feet, the only spot in the area where the silver ore came so close to the surface, they hit the vein of the fabulously wealthy mine they named the Little Pittsburgh. Tabor found himself one-third owner of a major producer and in short time, a millionaire.

For Tabor, a middle-aged stonemason from Maine who had tramped the Colorado mountains for 20 years, the find was the culmination of dreams of wealth and power. He invested the income from the Little Pittsburgh in even more productive strikes and gave away enormous sums to civic organiza-tions, which obsequiously named themselves in his honor, and built a gaudy array of buildings in Leadville.

But Leadville, the millionaire soon discovered, was not grand enough for the Tabor munificence. He wanted monuments to himself; and Denver, the

"GO BACKS" was the name given disgruntled Pikes Peakers who returned East. D. C. Oakes, an aspiring journalist who had written a guidebook touting the goldfields, once stopped at a new grave to find the epitaph: "Here lies the body of D. C. Oakes/Killed for aiding the Pikes Peak hoax."

budding town set where the golden grasslands joined the rise of the Shining Mountains, was a city to match his ambitions. In early 1879 he moved there.

Deprived of luxuries all his mean life, Tabor began to live in ostentatious splendor. When his acidic wife Augusta, a once-striking girl who began her marriage in a snake-infested Kansas soddy, refused to adjust to his grand style, he thrust her aside for blonde, girlish Baby Doe. After a scandalous divorce from Augusta, Tabor married Baby Doe in a Washington, D.C., ceremony attended by President Chester Arthur and a pride of politicos, whose smug wives stayed away. Then he brought her home to Denver and eventually to a $54,000-mansion on Capitol Hill where peacocks roamed the lawn.

Denver, which had existed barely long enough to have a second generation, was offended by the flatulent, foul-mouth storekeeper and his marital problems, but it was inordinately proud of the sensuously Victorian city he opened up. In quick succession Tabor erected the Tabor Block, the Tabor Grand Opera House, and helped the city secure the site for a post office, referred to as another "Tabor building."

GEN. WILLIAM LARIMER and his son Will built this ungainly cabin in 1858. Proud of his work, the general wrote his family: "You have no idea how nice Will and I are fixed up." (DPL)

Tabor was neither the first nor the best of the empire builders who lavished Denver with monuments, but he was the grandest, and his money was symbolic of the wealth that was to follow into the pretentious little supply center that was Denver. Tabor and the other silver kings took the infant Denver which tripled its population, from 36,000 in 1880 to 107,000 in 1890, and made it into a splendid city of imposing buildings and ostentatious homes. More important, the sometimes illiterate nouveaux riches gave Denver its exuberance, its supreme confidence, its style.

Twenty years earlier Tabor had been among the first to trek to Denver, a prairie settlement at the confluence of the South Platte and the Cherry Creek, that was known alternately as Auraria, St. Charles, and Coraville. It was started up in 1858 by a gold seeker named Green Russell, as much revered for the fact he plaited his beard as he founded the Rocky Mountains' greatest city.

Russell was followed by a scruffy crowd of fortune seekers, riff-raff, occasional murderers and thieves, and a smattering of what might be called founding fathers. Among them was General William Larimer, a sometime preacher, who, in setting a precedent religiously followed for more than one hundred years, never confused God and land development.

It was Larimer who called the settlement Denver, a name that finally

13

stuck, split the prairie with streets and building sites, and named the main thoroughfare "Larimer Street," immodestly for himself.

Denver represented a new type of Westward expansion in the United States. It was instant wealth, not land, that drew the settlers. Later came the more patient homesteaders, the sturdy sodbusters and plodding farmers who gave substance and religion and sensibility to the little towns. But the first frenzied arrivals at the city on the way to the Shining Mountains brought wheelbarrows to carry home the gold. Those who eschewed gold pans and picks contrived to make their fortunes with cards or con games or selling their souls, not a difficult task. And there was the merchant breed to service the little town, men like Count Henri Murat, a shirttail relative of the Emperor Napoleon, who opened Denver's first hotel, Uncle Dick Wootton, who arrived in time for Denver's first Christmas celebration with a wagonload of Taos Lightening and stayed on to become a businessman. And foppish Owen J. Goldrick, the dude with the boiled shirt and lemon-colored gloves, who swore in Latin so impressively he was given the job of the town's first schoolmaster.

There had been little reason for Denver's location. The settlement sprang up where it did because that was the spot Green Russell stopped to dip his pan in the stream. The South Platte and the Cherry Creek gave up little gold, however, and the prospectors soon wandered off to explore the gnarled mountain canyons to the west. But Denver was tough as whitleather. If it couldn't offer wealth, it would offer service. And prestige. When Colorado's miners hit paydirt, they deserted the mountain settlements to build the state's first cautiously Victorian mansions in Denver. It was unthinkable that Tabor, with his magnificent wealth, would settle elsewhere.

For its first 20 years, until Leadville silver began to pour into the city, Denver led a precarious existence. In 1863, a fire swept through the flimsy wood buildings and left Denver a charred mess, and a year later the placid Cherry Creek surged over its banks and flooded the rebuilt city. Indians had warned the gold seekers about the pretty stream lined with chokecherry trees, but settlers paid little attention, and the creek continued to flood at irregular intervals for seventy-five years.

More threatening to early Denver than fire or flood, however, was the threat of oblivion posed when the mighty Union Pacific Railroad announced it would lay its westward tracks through Cheyenne, Wyoming, 100 miles to the north, not through Denver. Since Denver was a mercantile center, the UP decision was critical, but Denver's emerging civic leaders organized to

Opposite page: YEAR-OLD DENVER was a proud city of raw buildings, mud streets, and squalid Indian settlements.

DENVER, 1859.

deal with it. Raising the money themselves, they built a connecting line to Cheyenne, and in 1870, patriarchial John Evans drove the final spike, linking Denver with the UP and survival.

The spike, ostensibly silver, was reportedly only iron, wrapped in white paper. Exuberant Denverites, legend says, were so proud of the rail hookup, they celebrated the night before in Mr. Charpiot's elegant restaurant on Larimer Street, and lost the silver spike. So they doctored up a plain one.

Tabor and the other high rollers who crowded into Denver—John Campion, the mining magnate; cattleman Dennis Sheedy; smelter king Nathaniel Hill; brewer John Good; and the banking Kountze brothers—enriched the city not only with their money, but with their taste, or what passed for it. They built mansions on Capitol Hill, recently platted by land developer Henry Brown, office buildings in downtown Denver, and spent their money with great abandon feasting on oysters at Mr. Pell's and magnums of champagne at Charpiot's. They got drunk at the 60-foot-long Windsor Hotel bar (and later the Brown Palace Hotel that Henry Brown built on an unsaleable

HANDBILLS of 1859 offered food, entertainment, clothes and other provisions, as well as legal services for those who needed them. (DPL)

EL DORADO HALL
AND
Restaurant,

J. G. SIMMS, Proprietor.

MEALS AT ALL HOURS.

THE TABLE

Will be supplied with the very best the market affords.

BOARD BY THE DAY AND WEEK.

Dispatch, neatness, and order, will always be observed.

GREAT PAINS TAKEN TO SECURE

GAME OF ALL KINDS.

THE BAR

Is supplied with a choice stock of pure Liquors and the finest Cigars.

A SPLENDID BILLIARD TABLE

Will be found by the lovers of this noble game.

Larimer street, bet. E & F streets,
DENVER CITY.

H. R. HUNT,
Attorney and Counsellor at Law,
AURARIA,

Tenders his professional services to the people of the Gold Regions.

CLAYTON, LOWE & CO.,
WHOLESALE AND RETAIL DEALERS IN

DRYGOODS, BOOTS, SHOES,
CLOTHING,
Gentlemen's Furnishing Goods,
GROCERIES,
Provisions, &c.

Store, S. W. corner Larimer and F streets,
DENVER CITY, K. T.

CHAS. R. MOREHEAD.   JOHN W. RUSSELL.

MOREHEAD & RUSSELL,
Dealers in

GROCERIES, PROVISIONS,
Wines, Liquors, Cigars, Tobacco, &c., &c.,
BLAKE STREET, DENVER CITY.

THE *Rocky Mountain News* was started in 1859 by William Byers, whose first edition came out only hours before a rival publisher was scheduled to begin printing a competitive paper. The loser gave up. (DPL)

cow pasture), and were fleeced by Soapy Smith, the most accomplished of con men. And they were solicitiously cared for by Mme. Mattie Silks, Mme. Jennie Rogers, and a covey of soiled doves in the opulent brothels that lined Market Street.

At the same time, Denver's middle class worked long hours in the dry goods stores or tiny factories, and rode home on the trolley instead of in carriages. On Saturday nights they drank nickel beer at dozens of saloons that crowded lower Denver; and on Sunday they stopped for ice cream sodas at O. P. Baur's fountain, which claimed to have invented the concoction. But there were certain equalities for them in the Democratic West; they, too, could get bilked by Soapy Smith.

Founded on gold, Denver blossomed in the late 1870s with the discovery of silver. When the bottom fell out of the silver market in 1893, with the repeal of the Sherman Silver Purchase Act, the city sank into a depression. Smelters closed, building fell off, banks failed, the local unit of Coxey's Army made plans to sail down the Platte, and the silver kings found them-

17

APOLLO HALL, second from left, was Denver's first legitimate theatre, opening in 1859 above a tumultuous gambling hall, with the forgettable play, "Cross of Gold." (DPL)

selves no longer able to afford finery at Daniels & Fisher or food for the peacocks in the front yard.

Hit by the silver crash, poor investments, and high living, Tabor lost everything but Baby Doe, who in the finest sense of Western melodrama, loved him more than his money, and stuck with him. When Tabor died in 1899, Baby Doe moved to the cabin of his Matchless Mine near Leadville, faithful to his prediction that silver would come back. It didn't, and she froze to death in the shafthouse 36 years later.

Denver was more fortunate than the Tabors. Gold was discovered at Cripple Creek, 100 miles to the south, and revived Colorado's—and Denver's—sagging fortunes. *Fin de Siecle* Denver was supported by gold from the far side of Pikes Peak and by emerging manufacturing and agricultural industries—beef, sugar beets, and cement—that were replacing Denver's mining oriented economy.

Denver's ambience changed, too, as the twentieth century dawned. Begun as a rough, rowdy settlement with a generous number of gin mills, gambling halls, and whorehouses—an early physician once wrote sourly that every

18

third man who reached the age of 25 had syphilis— it turned into a pretentious Victorian city wallowing in overblown architecture and refined sin. As Denver moved into the 1900s, age—it was a generation and a half old—stamped it with middle class values. Its people were more interested in parks than in pleasure palaces, in good working conditions than gold discoveries, and in improving the lot of the poor through institutional programs instead of charity baskets.

It became a city of white collar jobs and light industry. Small factories were opened—Samsonite Corporation, which manufactured luggage, and Gates Rubber Company. Founded in 1911, Gates was typical of Denver's paternalistically run companies. It organized exercise programs and sports teams, turned its factory roof into a garden, and in 1922 Mrs. Charles Gates, wife of the company founder, personally began buying Christmas presents for each of her "kiddies," the children of employees. In fact, until her death fifty years later, she ran the Gates Christmas party, the largest in the nation, where thousands of children received dolls and wagons and stuffed animals.

Not all Denver's children were as lucky as Mommie G's kiddies. Like other cities, Denver had its share of orphans and juvenile delinquents, but Denver was unique in dealing with them. Denver had Judge Ben Lindsey, an owlish, diminutive man of only 98 pounds, who was called, when he supported Theodore Roosevelt for president in 1912, "the Bull Mouse."

But his shadow was gargantuan. When he became a judge in 1900, Lind-

THE PROFUSION OF HOUSES could not hide Denver's bleak, treeless appearance in 1860. Tree planting started in earnest in 1865, when the city ditch began diverting water from the Platte for irrigation. (SHSC)

CLARK, GRUBER & CO. stamped out "mint drops," for use as local coins. They were more valuable than Civil War federal greenbacks, not backed by gold. (SHSC)

sey, outraged with the treatment of children arrested for petty crimes, campaigned for humane treatment of juveniles. Later he espoused easier divorce laws and even birth control.

Lindsey, who opposed private ownership of utilities, initiated child labor laws, fought the Ku Klux Klan, and in generally incurred the wrath of Denver's bribe-taking politicos, was shabbily ousted as judge and later moved to California.

Civic leaders in Denver could be as corrupt as elsewhere—and sometimes were—but curiously their personal greed could work in Denver's interest, and that was what happened with autocratic Mayor Robert Speer, who served the city on and off from 1904 to 1918. Speer's legacy to Denver is a magnificent park system, not just a block here and there decorated with civil war cannons, but vast tracts of land in Denver and the mountains filled with flower gardens, fountains, and expansive lawns. More than 50 years later, it seems inconsequential that he was accused of benefiting from the sale of some of the land the city condemned for civic use.

Denver entered World War I with the same chauvinism that gripped the rest of nation. Gates employees planted a victory garden behind the factory, the city organized parades, and shut down the whorehouses. Denver sent its finest to the trenches, and the newspapers whipped up patriotism.

In that era, Denver thrived as a journalists' city. F. G. Bonfils, a Kansas City con man, and Harry H. Tammen, whose notable achievement had been displaying petrified Moon-Eye, the Indian Maiden, to Denver's curious, teamed up in 1895, bought the placid *Denver Post,* and turned it into one of the country's flamboyant yellow sheets.

Journalism was as old as the city. William Byers started the *Rocky Mountain News* in an attic in 1859, and it has been published continuously since

THE ELEPHANT CORRAL, so called because of its ungainly size, was an iniquitous den where gambling went on 24 hours a day. *New York Tribune* editor Horace Greeley, touring the gold fields in 1859, made a strong anti-gambling, anti-drinking speech at the Elephant Corral (then called the Denver house) "which was received with perfect good humor," reported a journalist. (DPL)

DENVER'S timidly Victorian buildings had a sameness about their architecture, and only their uses varied: *Above,* the First National Bank Building under construction in 1865. The City Drugstore on the corner of 15th and Larimer (*top right*) must have been a photographer's haven. At the notorious Occidental (*center right*), where raunchy "Beer Girls" sold foul brew for 10 cents a glass, billiards was available, as was a reading room. Dry goods, furs, and other supplies were sold in the stores in the Fillmore Block (*below*), at the corner of Blake and 15th Streets. (SHSC-DPL)

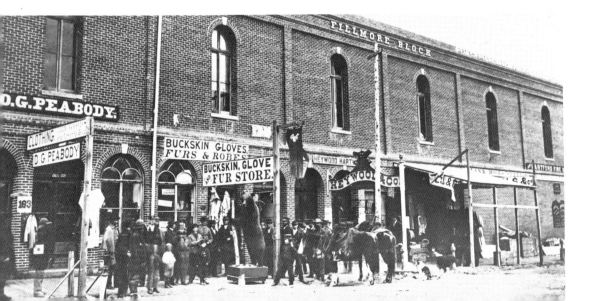

BIRKS CORNFORTH, by 1865, could boast an array of homegrown produce and a selection of foodstuffs freighted in from the East. (DPL)

then, except when one of those Cherry Creek floods inundated the print shop and carried off the press. (It was found years later, buried in the creek bed.)

Eugene Field, who later wrote maudlin children's poems, once was an editor on the *Denver Tribune* and a notorious practical joker, whose coup was impersonating Oscar Wilde. At one time or another Damon Runyan, Brooks Atkinson, and Gene Fowler were members of Denver's fourth estate. So were Polly Pry, Pinky Wayne, Mary Coyle Chase (author of "Harvey"), and Katherine Anne Porter, whose *Pale Horse, Pale Rider* was written about her World War I experiences as a reporter on the *Rocky Mountain News*.

Denver journalism reached its apogee under the tyranny of Bonfils and Tammen. They mercilessly flailed the mighty from their editorial room, known as the Bucket of Blood. And under their banner ". . . that no good cause shall lack a champion and that evil shall not thrive unopposed," they championed causes that were both just and good for circulation. In editorial frenzy, they attacked governors and water rates, undermined competition, and campaigned for the release from prison of Alferd Packer, gluttonous mountain guide who had devoured some of his friends during a snowstorm.

Good circulation created good profits, and the two owners of the *Post* moved into the Cheeseman Park area, which was replacing Capitol Hill as

DENVER'S FIRST FLOOD roared out of the Cherry Creek's banks in 1864, only a year after the city was charred by fire. (SHSC)

the city's most prestigious neighborhood. Tammen lived in a hulking, lavishly decorated mansion with a balcony designed especially for a Theodore Roosevelt speech, while Bonfils moved into a palazzo down the street with a balcony that served as a machine gun station during a threatened kidnapping.

Denver society of the war years, emerging from the rustic teaparty entertainments given by aging dowagers, was ruthlessly controlled by Mrs. Crawford Hill, whose father-in-law, Nathaniel Hill, had made his fortune with a process for extracting gold from ore. Louise Hill scandalized her elders by smoking and jumping into swimming pools and carrying on with a handsome younger man. But her parties were brilliant, and she was the indisputable leader of the Sacred 36—so called because 36 was the number required for nine tables of bridge.

Whenever Mrs. Hill entertained, Maggie Brown, stout boorish wife of James J. Brown, one-eighth owner of Leadville's Little Jonny mine, stood outside the Hills' iron fence, transfixed by the 36. She launched a ludicrous assault on Denver society, throwing parties in her garish home nobody attended, but not until she emerged the heroine of the *Titanic* disaster, keeping a boatload of people alive, did Mrs. Hill invite her to lunch. Little good it did her. Though to the world she was the Unsinkable Mrs. Brown, to Denver society she was simply the "Poor Unsinkable."

Life for both Maggie Brown and Louise Hill ended sadly. Maggie divorced her simple husband and ran through her money. And Mrs. Hill lived to be, as she told an embarassed dinner partner, "older than God," a senile old lady hidden away in a back room of the Brown Palace.

Denver society mostly ignored the social and political developments taking place during the 1920s and 1930s. The Ku Klux Klan made a whirlwind foray into Denver, organizing parades and cross-burnings and even controlled the legislature for a session in 1924, but a courageous group, made up of a handful of state senators, some civic leaders, and Judge Ben Lindsey, blunted the Klan's power.

The Great Depression hit Denver with less severity than elsewhere, a phenomenon that has existed since then during economic dips, due to Colorado's economic diversity. Still, Denverites dusted off gold pans in the attic and panned the South Platte, the Works Progress Administration set up shop, and the wealthy, spurred by noblesse oblige, erected mansions to give work to the needy and bravely carried on with an only slightly reduced standard of entertaining.

When Evalyn Walsh McLean, whose Croesus-like father had discovered the Camp Bird Mine in Western Colorado and set up his family in splendor in Washington, D.C., showed up at the Brown Palace one day, she managed

ARTIST A. E. MATHEWS took a whirlwind tour of Colorado in 1866, producing lithographs of what he saw. Viewed from the plains, Denver had a picturebook simplicity. (SHSC)

in a mere six hours, to recruit two name bands, a couple of ice elephants filled with caviar, a covey of roast Mexican quail, and Denver's finest families, for a little party. The bird-like Evie, who positively stooped under the weight of the Hope Diamond she slung around her neck, knew about depressions. At a lavish party in her enormous Washington home, only a few blocks from the Capital's breadlines, she overheard one bureaucrat, after surveying the dining table, murmur: "This is the sort of thing that causes revolutions."

The most famous Depression-era party was one from which Denver society was pointedly excluded. It was thrown for author Dorothy Parker, who had remarked she was tired of "stuffed shirts" and wanted to see some "real people" on her Denver visit. And so she did—pimps, prostitutes, the proprietor of a Chinese lottery, gamblers, and newspaper reporters. Denver's worst. Unfortunately, someone sent out bogus invitations to Denver society, which was unceremoniously turned away at the door. It was a smashing success anyway though the guests were served tea and ladyfingers, and many of them never had heard of the lionized little Mrs. Parker. "Jeeze," commented one of them, "who is this dame anyhow?"

Denver launched itself into World War II with the same generosity of spirit it rallied for other calamities. Once more the men volunteered, the women went off to manufacture munitions at a factory west of Denver, and the sanatorium on the east side of the city, which had drawn consumptives to the salubrious air of the West, was turned into Lowry Air Force Base. The soldiers trooped to Camp Carson, 80 miles south, or to the Leadville Mountains, where the army was training a select group of skiers as the 10th Moun-

LARIMER (not Laramie) Street shoppers had to contend with ankle-deep mud, carriages, stagecoaches, oxcarts, and fighting dogs. (DPL)

DENVER ELEGANCE, or what passed for it, was manifested in Ed Chase's Progressive gambling hall. The brass light fixtures and gilt-framed pictures were sorely out of place with wooden benches and plank floors. (DPL)

THE TAPPAN BUILDING was the tallest, hence the finest, office building in Denver when it was built in 1868.

tain Division. On leave, all of them poured into Denver. The city impressed them, and they in turn made a surprising impression on it. When the war was over, a stream of veterans came back to the city a mile above the sea.

But it was not the returning veterans who upset Denver as much as William Zeckendorf, the builder. Denver was still run by a dozen or so moldy, inbred families with ties back to the gold rush days. They ruled Denver sententiously from the stuffy Denver Club, a rustic stone building where unbridled excitement consisted of peering out the window at Maggie Brown overdressed in skunk skins, and wagging: "Here comes Colorado's unique fur bearing animal."

At the close of the war, Denver was, Zeckendorf declared, the town time forgot. Perhaps, but Denver's establishment liked it that way, and the satraps rallied against Zeckendorf when he announced he was buying the site of the old courthouse at the upper end of 16th Street and would build a hotel and retail complex on it. He did, but only after four years, 16 court actions, and bitter opposition.

When Denver's seneschals finally admitted defeat, Claude Boettcher, president of Ideal Cement Co., head of an investment firm, and an entrenched member of Denver's establishment, paid the developer a call.

"I come from the school of life that says when you lose to a man you don't fight him anymore," Boettcher told Zeckendorf. "You join him." It was the moment at which contemporary Denver was launched.

A PRIDE of lionized frontiersmen posed for a Denver photographer in the 1870's. left to right: William F. (Buffalo Bill) Cody, John B. Omahundro, James Butler (Wild Bill) Hickok, "Arapahoe Joe," and Charles H. Utter. (DPL)

FOREIGN ROYALTY considered the American West its private hunting preserve. Grand Duke Alexis of Russia, right, with George Armstrong Custer, hunted in Colorado territory, then turned prey to fortune hunting mothers when he attended a Denver ball in his honor. His manners were as boorish as his dancing, but so was Denver society in 1872. (DPL)

THE NOTORIOUS CRITERION SALOON was a hangout for the murderous gang run by Charlie Harrison, a Southern tough who once killed a black man for calling him by his first name. Later, as the Mozart Billiard Hall, it was tame enough for a harpist and balloon seller to hang out front. (DPL)

THE PALACE THEATRE had gambling room for 200, theatre space for 750. Among the customers were H. A. W. Tabor and Eugene Field. (DPL)

DANIELS, FISHER & CO. catered to a select clientele, splurging new found mineral fortunes on a wealth of goods imported from the East. (DPL)

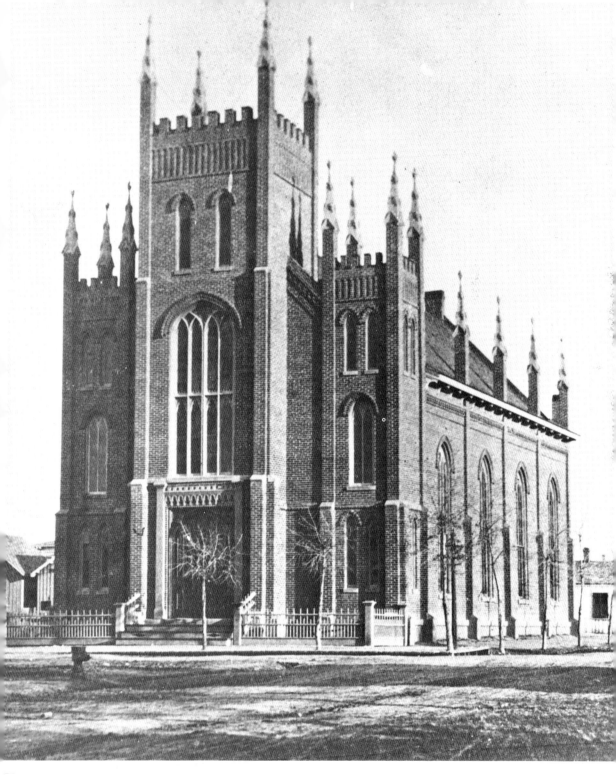

THE METHODISTS, who built the Lawrence Street Church, were a zealous lot, not always in the cause of God. Methodist preacher John M. Chivington butchered Indians with the same conviction he carried the word of God.

33

THE TABORS were Denver's most legendary triangle. When aging Horace Austin Warner Tabor (*above*) struck it rich, he divorced his dour wife Augusta (*center*) for Elizabeth Bonduel McCourt (Baby) Doe (*bottom*). (DPL)

34

The Boom Years (1879-1899)

THE TABOR MILLIONS helped turn Denver into a splendid Victorian city with construction of the massive Tabor Block, Denver's first skyscraper. (DPL)

THE TABOR GRAND OPERA HOUSE was described as "modified Egyptian Moresque" by arch critic, *Tribune* editor Eugene Field. He once wrote about an actress he abhorred: "Last night in front of the Tabor Theatre there drew up an empty cab, from which Mme. Bernhardt alighted." (DPL)

THE TABOR BOX was banked with lilies whenever Baby Doe attended a performance. (DPL)

THE FIRST TABOR HOME in Denver was this staid Victorian mansion. Augusta, suspicious of both Tabor's wealth and his affections, entered it reluctantly, remarking: "I will never go up those steps if you think I will ever have to go down them again." (DPL)

37

TABOR LATER ensconced Baby Doe in a more lavish home a few blocks away. (William Howland)

DENVER BOOMED under the largess of the silver kings. By 1882, the city had pleasant neighborhoods of middle-class houses and the pretentious beginning of an upper class enclave. The large building under construction (*above,* right) is the Arapahoe County Courthouse. (DPL)

THE WINDSOR HOTEL, conceived as modest family inn, got out of hand. It boasted diamond dust mirrors, marble floors, miles of Brussels, hand-carved furniture, in short, everything necessary to make it the most famous hostelry in the West. (SHSC)

THE "SUICIDE STAIRWAY" was a favorite departure point for once wealthy magnates who decided to end it all after the 1893 crash. H. A. W. Tabor died in 1899 in a back room of the Windsor, which by then was as second rate as he was. (DPL)

RESTAURANTS such as Pell's Fish House and Charpiot's "Delmonico of the West" served an amazing array of delicacies. Denverites were mad about oysters, and the city had half a dozen fish houses. Charpiot's was the scene of lavish parties and discrete trysts. And a dinner for four ran $7.00. (DPL-SHSC)

RAILROADS linked the city to both coasts, and without them, Denver would have been just another prairie village. The Union Depot was opened in 1881 to encourage passenger travel to Denver. It was gutted by an electrical fire in 1894. (DPL)

THE DENVER & RIO GRANDE maintained a splendid ticket office in a Larimer Street building. (DPL)

EASTERN IGNORANCE of the West's resources led to the establishment of the National Mining and Industrial Exhibition in 1882. The exhibition, which was supposed to be an annual event but was held only twice, displayed Colorado minerals and agricultural products. (DPL)

THIRTY-FOUR UTES set up teepees on the exhibition grounds. It was the first time Indians had been exploited as curiosities, and they rivaled only the bullion bricks in popularity. (DPL)

THE RICHTHOFEN CASTLE, built in 1883, was part of an ambitious East Denver suburb, Montclair, planned by the Baron Walter von Richthofen, a Prussian nobleman who was a relative of sorts of the Red Baron. (DPL)

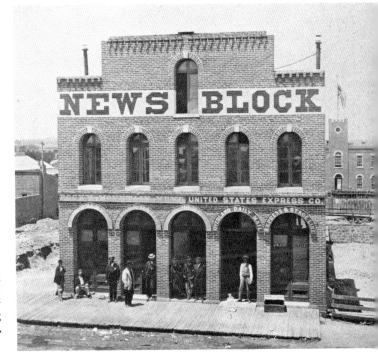

DENVER JOURNALISM, by the 1880s, had entered a period of bon vivance and pranksterism. Eugene Field was an editor on the *Denver Tribune* while dashing John Arkins managed the *News*. Asked by a reporter who was writing about potential sites for the World's Fair, "Where should the World's Fair be held?" Arkins replied: "Around the waist." (DPL)

DENVER HOMES might lack taste, but they never lacked imagination. (DPL)

MME. BELLA BERNARD operated this whorehouse on Market Street, already one of the famous fleshpot avenues of the West. (DPL)

LARIMER STREET was a bustling thoroughfare by the mid-1880s. The Tabor Block is at right, a series of gambling dens across from it, and the Windsor in the distant left. (DPL)

THE DENVER CLUB was the most sacrosanct of Denver institutions. From its strictly masculine confines, Colorado seneschals ruled the state. (DPL)

H. H. BUCKWALTER was an early balloonist who performed at Elitch Gardens. He later became an aerial photographer, using not an airplane but a balloon. (SHSC)

MARRIAGE IN A BALLOON may not have been the choice of many, but this couple, being married at what later became Elitch Gardens, found it the ideal send-off. Nobody recalls what happened to the airborne bridal pair. (SHSC)

47

AN ARRAY OF HOTELS tempted Denver visitors. The Inter-Ocean, built by black entrepreneur Barney Ford (*above*), boasted such modern features as an annunciator with wires to each room and a speaking tube on every floor. Still, *Ramona* author Helen Hunt Jackson called it "one of the most depressing places I have ever seen." The Markham, erected in 1872 (*below*), originally was three stories; the elegant fourth was added later The Albany, built in 1885 (*opposite page, top*), was a favorite gathering spot for cattlemen. (DPL-SHSC)

THE TORTONI, like other elegant restaurants catering to Denver big spenders, offered private dining rooms, where waiters knocked discretely before entering. (DPL)

MELTING SNOWS turned Denver streets into hog wallows. Denver got gaslights in 1871, electricity in 1880, but not until 1892 were the first downtown streets topped with asphalt. (DPL)

FEUDING QUEENS of Denver's red light district, Market Street, were babyish Mattie Silks (*right*) and elegant Jennie Rogers (*below*) Mme. Silks, who claimed she never had been a prostitute herself, arrived in Denver in the mid-1870s and operated almost until World War I. Mme. Rogers, who showed up shortly after Mattie, reportedly built her House of Mirrors, the plushest whorehouse from the Missouri River to the West Coast, by blackmailing a prominent businessman. (DPL)

50

CRIBS that lined upper Market Street housed most of Denver's prostitutes. Unlike the parlor house girls, the whores who operated out of Denver's rancid cribs were often drunkards or laudanum addicts. Murder and suicide, especially at Christmastime, were not uncommon. (DPL)

CAPITOL HILL, Henry Brown's land development, is in the foreground of this 1890 view of Denver. Grant Street, heart of Capitol Hill, already was being called "Millionaires Row" for the number of wealthy men who built homes there. (SHSC)

THE UNIVERSITY OF DENVER (a Methodist institution), right, Iliff School of Theology, left, and Loretto Heights College (a Catholic girls school), miles to the West, emphasized the Victorian belief that religion and education went hand-in-hand.

THE BROADWAY THEATRE, built in 1890, was a splendid setting for melodramas, prize fights, operatic performances, and plays, all of which were culture in Denver. (DPL)

DENVER UNIVERSITY'S Old Main was dedicated in a ceremony attended by loyal backers who rode special excursion trains to the site. The impoverished school paid early professors in building sites instead of money. (DPL)

LORETTO HEIGHTS, built at the same time, was dedicated to educating future wives and mothers in, among other things, "silence and modest reserve." (DPL)

CONSTRUCTION OF BELL TERRACE, at 14th and Bannock, one of Denver's upper middle class residential areas, drew a crowd of children. Despite a number of smart terraces and multi-family buildings, Denverites disdained apartment dwelling as only somewhat better than living above the store. (DPL)

A RAIN-DRENCHED CROWD watched the laying of the State Capitol cornerstone in 1890. The architecture is typical Victorian civic, with one special touch: the dome is gold plated. (SHSC)

THE COLORADO Mining Stock Exchange Building was the symbol of Colorado's mineral wealth. From his perch atop the Exchange, a 12-foot Colorado miner, pick in one hand, ore sample in the other, viewed Denver for 70 years. (DPL)

THE EQUITABLE BUILDING, erected in 1891, quickly became Denver's most prestigious office building. It still is. Its interior was lavished with Tiffany stained glass, mosaic work, vaulted ceilings, and "E's" on everything from the front door to the radiators.

THE H. C. BROWN PALACE, since the day it opened in 1892, has been Denver's most fashionable hotel. Its simple exterior belies its lavish interior, with an eight-floor rotunda, miles of onyx paneling, and a fireplace so immense it now is the entrance to a shop. (SHSC)

THE BROWN'S BATHROOMS were the delight of Coloradoans, who like other Victorians were infatuated with plumbing. (DPL)

JEFFERSON ("SOAPY") SMITH was an inspired con man who fleeced Denverites with freak shows (*below*) and a school to cure gamblers. His name came from an early bilk in which he sold bars of soap at several times the market price by claiming some of them had hundred dollar bills inside the wrappers. (DPL)

A WONDER

--- THE ---

PETRIFIED MAN

Discovered near Creede, Colo., April 9, 1892.

A petrifaction as natural as life, showing a fine specimen of manhood; every muscle, and even the pores of the skin are plainly seen by the naked eye. Parts of the petrifaction have been analyzed by the most skeptical, and it has been pronounced genuine by all. **$1,000** to any one proving to the contrary. Skeptics, Doctors and all Scientific men are especially invited.

ON EXHIBITION AT

914 SEVENTEENTH ST,

Admission, 10 Cents.

THE CITY HALL WAR erupted in 1894 when Gov. Davis H. ("Bloody Bridles") Waite called out the state militia to forcefully evict political appointees he had dismissed. Despite the troops outside, the officials and their gunslingers within, and the crowd of spectators, nobody was hurt. Waite got his "Bloody Bridles" sobriquet not from the City Hall War but from a defiant statement he made shortly before the repeal of the Sherman Silver Purchase Act, warning Wall Street of rebellion. Said Waite: "It is better, infinitely better, that blood should flow to the horses' bridles rather than our national liberties should be destroyed." (DPL)

THE ARAPAHOE COUNTY COURTHOUSE, begun in 1881 and built in two installments, cost the taxpayers less than $500,000. The building was torn down fifty years later and the land subsequently acquired by William Zeckendorf. (SHSC)

BAM MATTS DIAMOND

PHOTO BY C McCLURE, DENVER

DENVER ENTREPRENEURS were an enterprising lot, offering an amazing array of merchandise, much of which had to be imported from the East. A shopper could choose from hundreds of tonsorial items at Buerger Brothers (*below*), a stunning selection of jewels at Sam Mayer's Diamond Palace (*opposite page*), or a variety of meats and wild game at Leikauf's (*above*). (DPL)

63

THE FESTIVAL of the Mountain and Plain was started in 1895 by a city thankful that Cripple Creek gold was pouring into her coffers, relieving the depression caused by repeal of the Sherman Silver Purchase Act. It was repeated fitfully until 1912. Highlights of the festivals were the parades with elaborate floats, displays of produce and manufactured goods, bands, and of course queens. (DPL-SHSC)

FESTIVAL
OF MOUNTAIN AND PLAIN
DENVER
AND
STATE
FAIR
SEPT. 25 TO 30
1899
SLAVES
of the SILVER SERPENT.
A. TEN WINKEL
Low Rates on all Railroads.
THE Williamson-Haffner Eng. Co
DENVER, COLO.

THE GUMRY HOTEL was destroyed in 1895 when a boiler exploded, killing 22 people. The boiler room engineer had gone out for a beer. (SHSC)

BICYCLE RACERS were the terror of the highways and the temptation of young women. Here the Fire Underwriters hold their first road race, in 1895. (DPL)

CROWDS AT THE DENVER STOCK EXCHANGE emphasized the growing maturity of Denver businessmen. They were becoming sophisticated investors and, indeed, stock manipulators, too. (DPL)

THIRTY-SEVEN is a heavy load for the Denver Omnibus and Cab Co., a sightseeing operation, even with six horses. (DPL)

THE DENVER ATHLETIC CLUB was formed in 1884, ostensibly to promote physical fitness for gentlemen. It also promoted good times, not necessarily for gentlemen. (DPL)

EVERY DRUGSTORE had a soda fountain, dispensing phosphates at five cents a glass. White & McMahan's Drugstore was at 21st Street and Larimer. (DPL)

THE INTER-OCEAN CLUB, located in what had once been the opulent home of merchant W. B. Daniels, was operated by Ed Chase, who had opened the Palace early in Denver's history. Its room arrangement was so confusing that, during a raid, the management generally was able to hide gambling evidence before the law found the gaming rooms. (Mazzulla)

69

PHOTOGRAPHERS covered Denver's life virtually from its birth. The most famous was patriarchial William H. Jackson, who maintained this studio. L. C. McClure, second from right, later went out on his own, photographing Denver for thirty years. (DPL)

SATURDAY NIGHT BEER DRINKING was a favorite pastime despite periodic prohibition efforts. The Coors sign, left, is evidence the West's most popular beer was already catching on. (DPL)

ZANG'S BEER "that made Colorado famous" was another favorite drink, at five cents a glass. For a mere 20 cents, a man could have four beers or a room for the night. (DPL)

TIVOLI was a third popular beer. Both Tivoli and Zang's Beer are gone. (DPL)

THE WOMAN'S Christian Temperance Union was a formidable opposition to Demon Rum in Denver. (DPL)

NATURE'S CURE did have its advocates, but mountain men hardly were among them. (SHSC)

NEARLY 18,000 miles of wire, most of it in Denver linked the state's telephone subscribers. (Mt. Bell)

TELEPHONE SERVICE was started in 1879, with 200 subscribers and a host of detractors who questioned the usefulness of the device. By the end of the century, 45,000 calls were being made daily on the city's 4,500 phones. (Mt. Bell)

Two mercantile establishments that appealed to Denver's well-to-do were the May Co., founded in Leadville, Colo., and Daniels & Fisher Stores Co. (*below*). The stores gave special service to certain customers, dispatching a clerk with merchandise to show to Baby Doe in her carriage, or overcharging prostitutes. The two stores merged in 1958. (DPL)

Settling In (1900-1920)

THE EQUITABLE BUILDING is the tall structure on the left in this turn-of-the-century photograph of 17th Street, which for more than 75 years has been Denver's financial heart—if one assumes Denver financiers have a heart. (DPL)

THE BIGGEST FLAG in the world, or so Daniels & Fisher, the plush department store, claimed when it unfurled it in 1905, was flown for parades and tourist conventions. It was too heavy to hang from a flag pole. (DPL)

THE DENVER STREET CLEANING DEPARTMENT was called the "white wings," for the jackets worn by its broom-sweeping brigade.

OVERLAND PARK, so named because one had to go "over land" from Denver to get there, was Denver's first golf course. No dogs nor tips were allowed at the clubhouse. (DPL)

ELITCH GARDENS claims the country's oldest summer stock theatre, and has featured stars ranging from Sarah Bernhardt to Grace Kelly. Douglas Fairbanks, a Denver schoolboy, once scrubbed the stage in exchange for a theatre ticket. (DPL)

THE ELITCH THEATRE curtain was a pretentious scene of Anne Hathaway's cottage. "Anne" was misspelled "Ann," but no matter. Some of the theatre goers still couldn't read. (DPL)

THE MINIATURE TRAIN was part of an elaborate midway that grew up around the Elitch Theatre and its flower gardens. (DPL)

THE HORSE-DRAWN CHERRELYN CAR operated on a reciprocal agreement. The horse pulled the car uphill, then climbed aboard and rode down. (DPL)

THE GEORGE F. WATROUS CAFE was one of dozens of lunchroom operations that provided daily bread for Denver workers. (DPL)

THE NAVARRE was the last of Denver's elegant gambling palaces operated by the aging though undauntable Ed Chase. It offered a side entrance for ladies and private dining rooms. (DPL)

"BUCKING THE TIGER," a painting at the Navarre. (Mazzulla)

80

PRESIDENT THEODORE ROOSE-
VELT was a Colorado regular, who
toured mining camps, visited politicos,
and hunted in the Colorado mountains.
The "teddy bear" reportedly got its name
from a bear Roosevelt shot near Glen-
wood Springs, Colorado. Other U. S. lo-
cales claim the same story. This parade
took place in 1903. (DPL)

FEMININE PASTIMES, in an era of in-
creasing leisure for the middle class,
ranged from painting mountain scenes on
buckskin pillows to cycling around the
City Park Lake. One dressed for both
occasions. (DPL)

81

ANY EVENT, even a state fair, was reason for a parade. (DPL)

AARON GOVE, an architect, and his family were typical of Denver's rising middle class. (DPL)

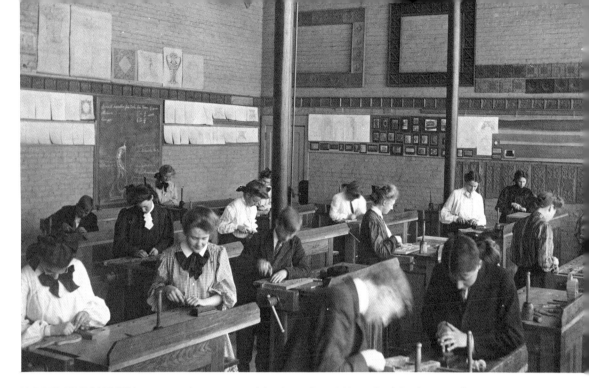

HIGHER EDUCATION for many students meant training for crafts and blue collar jobs. A group of students learn carving at Manual High School. (DPL)

MANUAL HIGH SCHOOL'S volleyball team was the terror of the courts. (DPL)

A COLLISION of two eras, between the Indian whose world had faded, and that modern miracle the automobile, whose day was just dawning. (DPL)

AUTOMOBILES fascinated Denverites. William Hover, who received Denver's first automobile permit, is about to take off down 12th Avenue with a daring group of clergymen. (DPL)

THE HAZARDS of Sunday driving on the prairie outside Denver are all too clear to this family. (DPL)

ONE BENEFIT of the horseless carriage—it would soon take necking out of the park and put it in the back seat where it belonged. (DPL)

TOURING BY CAR was highly fashionable when these two ladies posed for a souvenir shot. (DPL)

MOTORIZED BUSES, zooming about the city, followed close on the dust of Denver's first automobiles. (DPL)

MARKET STREET at 15th was the center of Denver's wholesale trade. Horsecarts remained the chief mode of transportation despite the advent of automobiles. (DPL)

IN HUCK-FINN BEGUILINGNESS, a group of children pose for a photographer in Berkeley Park. (DPL)

EVERY SCHOOLBOY'S IDOL was Buffalo Bill Cody, the great Pahaska, as renowned for his liquor consumption as his prowess as an Indian fighter. When Cody's doctor limited him to a parsimonious 10 drinks a day, Cody solved the dilemma by taking each drink in a beer glass. (DPL)

EN ROUTE

AGAIN WE GREET YOU

And this time with the GREATEST DRAMATIC ATTRACTION ever presented to a Theatre Going Public. Most Extraordinary Success has attended

THE ILLUSTRIOUS GOVERNMENT SCOUT,

BUFFALO BILL

SIOUX CHIEFS!

SIOUX CHIEFS!

(HON. W. F. CODY,) AND HIS

COMBINATION

During their recent visits to PHILADELPHIA, BALTIMORE, WASHINGTON and NEW YORK, where, even the largest Opera Houses have been incapable of accommodating the masses, and in which latter city a re-engagement was made at the New and Capacious EAGLE THEATRE, which was packed nightly with the elite,

To witness the Most Refined and Meritorious SENSATIONAL DRAMA ever written, entitled

MAY CODY

OR, LOST AND WON.

Written expressly for Hon. W. F. CODY (Buffalo Bill) by MAJ. A. S. BURT, U.S.A.

THE WELCOME ARCH at Union Station greeted railroad visitors for years. On the other side was the word "Mizpah," which meant a meeting place of ancient Hebrews. (DPL)

TRAINS were the most popular means of transportation, whether one rode coach or in one of the lavish private cars that frequently were parked on Denver's siding. (SHSC)

BUILT by the Walter Cheesman family, this house later was home of Denver business leader Claude K. Boettcher. Today, crammed with antiques which seem to have been collected for their panache rather than their aesthetic value (i.e., a chandelier from the White House), the house is Colorado's governors mansion. (DPL)

89

HUMBOLDT STREET was becoming the new "Millionaires Row." Gov. William Sweet resided in the corner house. Next door lived *Denver Post* owner and circus magnate Harry Tammen, who in a fit of pique at his neighbor once threatened to place the stuffed carcass of his favorite elephant in the back yard. (DPL)

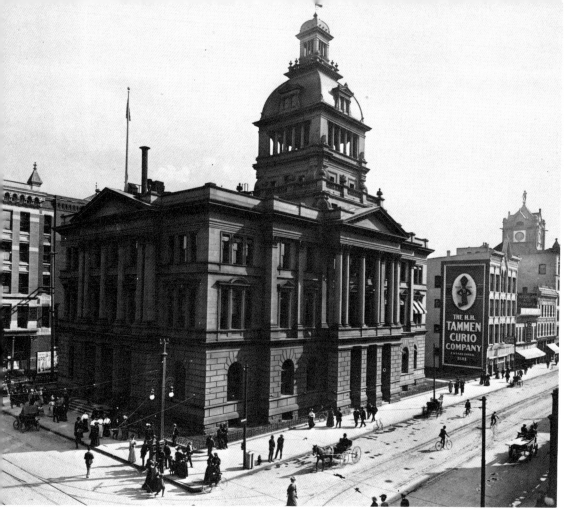

THE DENVER FEDERAL BUILDING, was built on land purchased from H. A. W. Tabor, who later worked there after his luck played out. Next door, *Denver Post* owner Harry Tammen, who never got over his sideshow proclivities, maintained a curio company. (DPL)

Facing Page: DENVER from 16th Street and Arapahoe. The Tabor Grand is at right. (DPL)

THESE SMARTLY DRESSED statehouse clerks were caught in a spring storm. (DPL)

THE CITY AUDITORIUM, built just in time for the Democratic National Convention to nominate William Jennings Bryan in 1908, was little more successful than the Presidential candidate. The hulking auditorium with its poor acoustics never has been a Denver favorite. (DPL)

TAMMANY still was a powerful influence in the 1908 Democratic convention. (DPL)

EXERCISE WANDS and dumbbells were part of the daily physical fitness program at Gilpin School. So were exercises on the horizontal bars. (DPL)

IN MOCK RECALCITRANCE, two Gilpin boys pose for a photographer with a birds' nest and what appears to be a cardboard bird. The photographer's shadow is in the foreground. (DPL)

DAMON RUNYAN, shown with Jim Wong at the Denver Press Club, was a Denver journalist before he became an author. Some of his characters were drawn from Denver people. (DPL)

PRESIDENT WILLIAM HOWARD TAFT stopped to hug two little girls during his 1909 Denver trip. (DPL)

THE PRESIDENT motored to the Wolhurst estate to lunch with the Walsh family. Evalyn Walsh (McLean), holding the puppy, later became a Washington socialite and confidante of the Hardings. (DPL)

THE LAWRENCE STREET Methodist Church, where early Denver prayed for salvation, was a Salvation Army outpost in 1909. (DPL)

THE SELLS FLOTO CIRCUS was organized by Harry Tammen to promote the *Denver Post* and to fulfill his schoolboy dream of owning a circus. Reportedly, local nabobs were forced, through threat of editorial blackmail, to buy shares called "monkey stock," in the circus. (DPL)

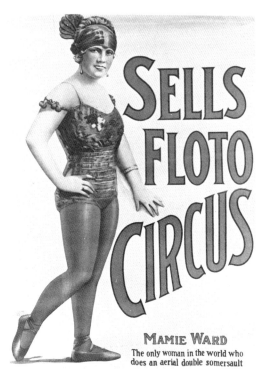

LAKESIDE, "the White City," complete with midway, ballroom, and breath-taking rides, was opened to compete with Elitch Gardens. (DPL)

SUMMER OR WINTER, City Park Lake met Denverites' growing passion for outdoor sports. (DPL)

THE GREAT WHITE WAY was Curtis Street, where theatres such as the Isis (*below*) and the Princess (*right*) attracted throngs of enthralled movie goers. (DPL)

DRINKING, from the city's inception, was a particularly pleasant way of passing the evening, whether you were a young blood in the smart Brown Palace Bar (*above*) or a family man. The room, with its matching golden oak furniture, canary, and cloying tapestry, is as stiff as the cigar smoking bourbon drinker. (DPL)

BALLOON TRAINING was part of maneuvers for the Colorado National Guard Signal Corps in 1909. (SHSC)

ROSE MARY ECHO Silver Dollar ("Honeymaid") Tabor, Baby Doe's daughter, presented a copy of a song she wrote to President Theodore Roosevelt on one of his Colorado trips. She lived a sordid life, and was scalded to death in a Chicago hotel room. (DPL)

THE DOUDS, at 750 Lafayette, were a typical upper-middle class family, except that little Mamie, holding the rabbit (standing at the top of the steps) would marry Dwight Eisenhower and become the country's first lady. (DPL)

99

DENVER IN 1911 was showing middle-age spread. The first mansions already were boarding houses, suburbs were springing up, and trees had reached respectable size on the once barren prairie (*also facing page at left*) (DPL)

101

A RECORD-BREAKING BLIZZARD hit Denver in 1913, stopping trolleys in the streets and stranding hundreds of workers in downtown office buildings. (DPL)

THE CITY HAULED snow to the Civic Center, where it remained until spring thaw. (DPL)

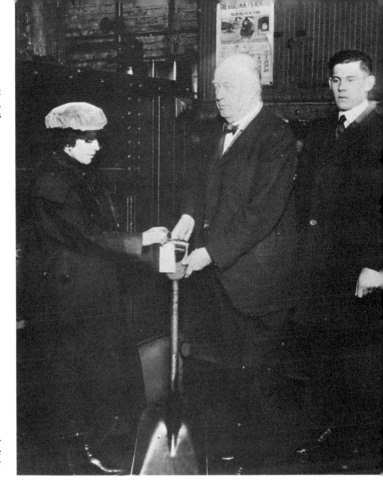

MAYOR ROBERT SPEER, shown at one of his innumerable groundbreakings, was responsible for Denver's parkways and city parks. (DPL)

RED ROCKS, a natural sandstone outcropping west of Denver, was one of the areas preserved in Mayor Speer's Denver Mountain Parks system. (DPL)

THE DANIELS & FISHER TOWER, built in 1911, was patterned after the Campanile of St. Mark's Square in Venice. Standing at 16th Street and Arapahoe, it is Denver's best-known landmark. (DPL)

MRS. J. J. (MAGGIE) BROWN, better known as "The Unsinkable Mrs. Brown," an overbearing social climber who dressed outlandishly, sometimes in skunk skins, longed to be accepted by Denver's social Sacred 36. When the *Titanic* hit an iceberg on its maiden voyage in 1912, she kept a lifeboat of people alive, and remarked later: "I'm unsinkable." (DPL)

MRS. CRAWFORD HILL, leader of the Sacred 36 (shown with her sons), refused to accept Maggie Brown's invitations, and asked her for lunch only after she became a national celebrity. (DPL)

THE HILL MANSION was hopelessly alluring for Maggie Brown, who would stand beside the iron fence for hours watching the Hill guests come and go. (DPL)

MAGGIE'S HOME was oppressively decorated for her parties. Despite official rejection by the Sacred 36, Maggie, because of her generosity and wit, made a number of friends among lesser society. When she ran into a Denver friend who had booked passage on the *Titanic* but at the last minute had changed her plans, Maggie trumpeted: "Oh, you should have been there. We had such an exciting time." (DPL)

PLAYGROUNDS and other recreational facilities were an important part of Denver's parks, which do not have "keep off the grass" signs. (DPL)

THE ZOO at City Park, begun with a few rangy animals, has increased to impressive proportions. (DPL)

FREDERICK BONFILS (*right*) and Harry Tammen were a conniving, flamboyant pair who turned the tepid *Denver Post* into a sensational newspaper. (DPL)

PROMOTIONS AND GIVE-AWAYS by the *Denver Post,* designed to boost circulation, drew hundreds of people to the *Post* building (*below left*). The *Post* never missed a good act—even magician Harry Houdini was persuaded to hang from a sign in front of the *Post* building. (DPL)

109

THE KNIGHTS TEMPLAR held their 1913 convention in Denver. In case anybody missed them, the group built this symbol of itself near the post office. (DPL)

TWO ACTRESSES REHEARSE for a performance of "Salvation Nell" at Elitch Gardens. Viewing the play, strong men winced when an actor muttered "God damn" on stage, and the *Post* reporter said he'd rather take his daughter on a tour of Market Street whorehouses before letting her attend a performance. Her preference was not recorded. (DPL)

THE TABOR GRAND offered comedies, vaudeville acts, and movies, after traveling thespians such as Lily Langtree and Sarah Bernhardt played out. Peter McCourt, manager, was Baby Doe's brother. (SHSC)

STRENGTH was one of the virtues of Samsonite Corp.'s trunks and suitcases, made in Denver. Samsonite is the country's largest manufacturer of luggage. (Samsonite)

THE WHOLE FAMILY tried out this one. The family: The Shwayders, who ran Samsonite from its founding in 1910 until its acquisition by Beatrice Foods Co. in 1973. (Samsonite)

GATES RUBBER CO. founded in 1911, was typical of Denver's paternalistic companies. (Gates)

BESIDES WORKING, employees exercised and even improved their minds. (Gates)

THE COMPANY, which originally made V-belts and then branches into hoses and tires, now owns a mutual fund management and insurance company, a freight line, and controlling interest in Gates Learjet Corp. (Gates)

MATTIE SILKS (at left), doyenne of the red light district until her death in 1929, never outgrew her love of good flesh—male, female, or horse. (DPL)

114

BATHING BEAUTIES at Berkeley Park Lake drew admiring glances with their daring swimming suits and rolled down stockings. The lady on the left appears oblivious to the hole in her stocking. (DPL)

FISHING in nearby mountain streams
was another way of spending the week-
end. (DPL)

DENVER WENT TO WAR with the rest of the country, sending its boys to fight Germany, knitting socks, and organizing parades. (DPL)

PATRIOTIC GATES EMPLOYEES tended a victory garden adjacent to the rubber company. (Gates)

WOMEN STREETCAR CONDUCTORS took over for men, who had gone off to fight the Kaiser. They were ousted from their jobs as soon as the soldiers came back. (DPL)

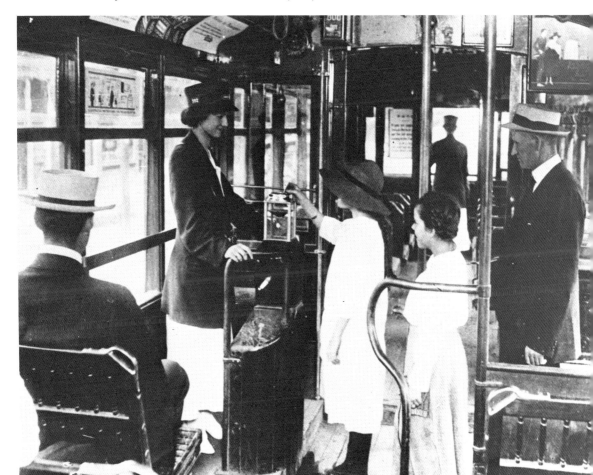

JUDGE BEN LINDSEY advocated compassionate child laws and established a Juvenile Court that was widely copied. It received wide support, particularly from those who as children had benefited from Judge Lindsey's humane treatment. He offended too many people, however, and was disbarred. (DPL)

BUFFALO BILL CODY was an institution, denounced as a faker and a drunk by some, and acclaimed as the last frontiersman by others. Whatever he was, Buffalo Bill was universally loved by little children. (DPL)

BITTER AND BROKE, Buffalo Bill died in 1917 and was buried on Lookout Mountain, west of Denver. His funeral was the success his Wild West Show once had been. Two states fought over the body, and an aging bevy of once beguiled beauties, black-clad, were overcome with grief all through the ceremony. (SHSC and DPL)

PRESIDENT WOODROW WILSON, accompanied by Colorado Governor Oliver Shoup, visited Denver in 1919. (DPL)

DENVER PAVING EQUIPMENT chugs up 16th Street. The Arapahoe County Courthouse is at left. (DPL)

Queen City of the Plains (1921-1945)

THE SERENITY of Capitol Hill belied the fact the world was about to enter the jazz era. (DPL)

D&F'S TOWER loomed up in almost any downtown picture taken after 1911, and it played a part in many lives. Shopgirls attended school in the tower, and school children paid a few cents to ride the elevator to the top for a dizzying view of Denver. (DPL)

THE DENVER TRAMWAY STRIKE of 1920 pitted streetcar employees against scabs in a series of clashes that climaxed when trolleys were smashed and overturned in front of Immaculate Conception Cathedral. That evening, the *Denver Post,* never neutral, was ransacked. (SHSC)

IMMACULATE CONCEPTION, in more serene times, assuaged the souls of Denver Catholics. (DPL)

DENVER'S POPCORN SET was en-thralled with movie making and viewing. The forgettable "Miss Arizona" was filmed locally, though it was hardly as popular as the provocative "Men Who Have Made Love to Me," which played at the America Theater. (DPL)

ENRICO CARUSO performed in "Girl of the Golden West," which bore about as much resemblance to the real West as Ca-ruso did to a cowboy. (DPL)

THE MERRY-GO-ROUND at Overland
Park was as good a place as any to spend
a Sunday afternoon if you were a kid. The
"bump cars" at Lakeside were even better
if you were a big sister. (DPL)

DENVER'S FINEST were still dependent on horses and bicycles in 1920. Here the Capitol Hill Station crowd poses with three of its three-wheeled crime-catchers, complete with sidecars. (DPL)

SPEEDING TICKETS were a hazard for early drivers, who scarcely could outrace Denver's mounted patrolmen. (DPL)

FIRES, except for the big blaze of 1863, were never much of a problem in Denver. Local fire fighters had to content themselves with conspicuous pumping displays, or posing aboard their spit-and-polish pumpers. (DPL)

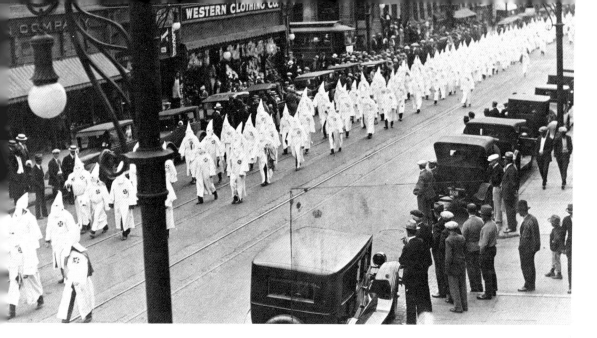

THE KU KLUX KLAN made a strong showing in Colorado's 1924 elections but failed to steamroll through pet programs, such as an anti-Catholic bill to forbid the use of wine in religious services. Highly visible Klan parades and cross burnings lasted only a few years. (DPL)

DENVER'S EMANCIPATED WOMEN took to strenuous sports, such as golfing at the municipal golf links in Bear Creek Canyon, or mountain climbing at Red Rocks, one of the city-owned mountain parks. (DPL)

128

MALE SPORTING BLOODS preferred trap shooting at Sloans Lake or polo, a sport popularized by the Anglophiles who lived in Colorado Springs' "Little London." (DPL)

GYPSY MOTORIST, as tourists were called, crowded into Overland Park camp-ground. The clubhouse, remodeled in 1921, contained a grocery store, soda fountain, dance hall with Victrola music, and even a public laundry. (DPL)

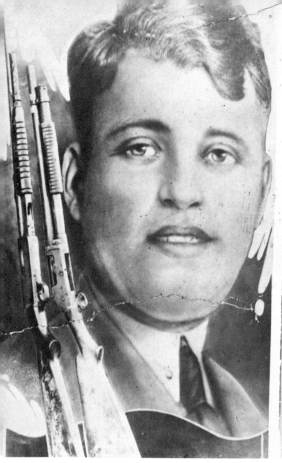

THE $200,000 DENVER MINT ROB-BERY in 1922, resulted in the death of a guard and one of the robbers, J. S. Sloan (*above*) whose frozen body was found two weeks later in a car. Only part of the money was ever recovered. (DPL)

"DIAMOND JACK," a combination Colorado cowboy and gangster, was executed in 1935 in gangland style. (DPL)

PRIZE FIGHTER Jack Dempsey, the famed Manassa Mauler (from Manassa, Colo.) and his wife Maxine were Denver visitors. Dempsey once was a mucker in a Cripple Creek mine. (DPL)

VIRILE COWBOYS and noble Indians had disappeared by the mid-1920s except in Wild West shows, such as this one at Overland Park. Or maybe they never had existed at all. (DPL)

MOTORCYCLISTS by the 1920s had replaced bicycle racers as sex symbols. Well, sort of. (DPL)

BAUR'S RESTAURANT, which claims invention of the ice cream soda, was an elegant soda fountain and candy store, decorated with marble, angel heads, and hand-painted murals. (DPL)

132

DENVER BUSINESS in the 1920s was benevolently ruled by the 17th Street crowd, which operated from the First National Bank (*left*) and the Colorado National Bank (*above.*) (First Natl.-DPL)

BUSINESS DEALS were settled over luncheon in the Brown Palace dining room or in the hotel's massive rotunda, awesome not only because it rose eight stories but because, even during the 1929 crash, nobody ever commited suicide by jumping over a railing. (DPL)

OVERLAND PARK AUTO RACES, held on a track originally used for harness racing, drew home-made race cars. The last race was held in 1925--100 times around the one-mile track for a purse of $10,000. (DPL)

CHICAGO'S LADY SINGING ORCHESTRA, with powdered wigs and pennants, were part of a Dutch Mill Restaurant promotion. (DPL)

EVANGELISTS Aimee Semple McPherson and Billy Sunday administered to the Denver multitudes in the fertile revival period of the 1920s. Socialite Crawford Hill once tried to have the site of a Billy Sunday service changed because it was too close to his home. (DPL)

135

QUEEN MARIE OF RUMANIA, setting out from Union Station in 1926, enthralled Denver as had royalty since Grand Duke Alexis. (DPL)

Preceding page: THE CIVIC CENTER complex, envisioned by Mayor Speer, was a six block area that included the State Capitol, City and County Building, the Denver Public Library, a Greek amphitheatre, colonnades, and formal gardens. (DPL)

CHARLES A. LINDBERGH flew the Spirit of St. Louis into Denver in 1927. Amelia Earhart (*above*), shown with aging Frederick Bonfils, arrived a year later. (DPL)

DENVER UNION AIRPORT, at 52nd and Cherry, was one of half-a-dozen airfields near present day Stapleton International Airport. Sunbeam was a fledgling airline started about 1930 with four airplanes. It ended when its financial backer was killed in an airplane crash. (DPL)

LOWRY FIELD, named for Lt. Francis Brown Lowry, only Denver flier to lose his life in World War I, was another local flying field. The name later was used for an Air Force base. (Lowry)

THE GATES HALF SOLES, with mascot and batboys, was part of the corporate sandlot league. Charles C. Gates, company founder, is in the center. (Gates)

BABY DOE TABOR walked Denver streets almost unnoticed on her infrequent trips to the city to get financing for her Matchless Mine. She always wore a cap, perhaps to hide her hair, which was a glorious gold until she died: (DPL)

"THE HOUSE THAT GRAFT BUILT," as it was then irreverently called, the City and County Building was erected in 1931. (DPL)

CIVIC CENTER CHRISTMAS decorations, which have become more garish each year, are, like floods and rattlesnakes, Denver tradition. (DPL)

GREEK ARCHITECTURE hardly was indigenous to the prairie city, but Denverites basked in the auspiciousness of the Voorhies Memorial and Greek Amphitheatre. (DPL)

THE 1933 FLOOD hit Denver with vengeance, inundating Union Station, destroying shops, and turning neighborhood streets into canals. Completion of the Cherry Creek Dam several years later finally kept the fickle trickle within its banks. (DPL)

DENVER RADIO STATIONS were quick to seize promotional tie-ins. From its prominent box at the long-gone City Park track, KGHF broadcasts a horse race. KVOD, whose call letters recently have resurfaced, broadcast Uncle Jim's Question Bee, sponsored by your neighborhood Save-a-Nickel stores. (DPL)

TOM MIX visited Denver in 1931. (DPL)

THE TROLLEYS linked every part of Denver and its suburbs. Generations of Denverites rode them to work, to church, and to the city's numerous parks. (DPL)

DENVER'S YOUNG TOUGHS gather under one of the city's viaducts. (DPL)

WPA SOUP KITCHENS accommodated those who were not fortunate enough to be Gates kiddies. (DPL)

MOMMIE G'S KIDDIES fared well during the Depression. Hundreds of children received Christmas presents from the wife of the founder of Gates Rubber Co. Each gift was marked with the recipient's name. The parties took weeks to plan, and required elaborate record keeping. (Gates)

THE WORKS PROGRESS ADMINISTRATION provided hundreds of jobs for the unemployed. Workers undertook numerous building projects in Denver, including this storm sewer, and artist and writers recorded the state's history. The pictures are of H. A. W. and Augusta Tabor and the Tabor mansion. (DPL)

SLUICING AND GOLD PANNING the South Platte was a familiar sight during the Great Depression. (DPL)

GOOD TIMES were hardly there when the Orpheum opened in the midst of the Depression, but the theater did at least help the unemployed forget their plight for a few hours. (DPL)

GOLF at the Denver Country Club was another depression era panacea. (DPL)

THE RICH did their part to help offset the effects of the Depression by building mansions. The Phipps family built its Bel-caro home (*left*), to give work to the unemployed. The Weckbaughs had the same idea in mind (*below*), when they built their Country Club chateau. (DPL)

148

EVALYN WALSH MCLEAN, with the Hope diamond dangling around her neck, threw a full dress party at the Brown Palace with a mere six hours notice. The city's best turned out, including Denver historian Caroline Bancroft, and Lucius Beebe, author and bon vivant. (Caroline Bancroft)

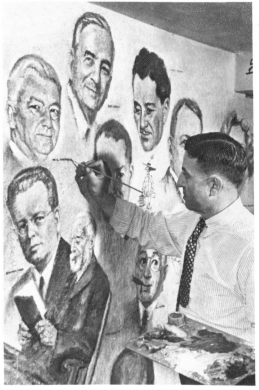

FRANK HAMILTON RICE (with clerical collar) organized the Liberal Church, dedicated to the undeserving, after his Methodist congregation opposed teenage dancing in the church and his attitude toward rational sex ethics. Rice celebrated communion with near-beer and ordained bums as ministers so they could beg legally. (DPL)

HERNDON DAVIS (*right*) painted pictures of Colorado newsmen on the walls of the Denver Press Club. Upper right: Lowell Thomas, lower right: Eugene Field. Herndon Davis is best known for painting the face on the floor of Central City's Teller House barroom. (DPL)

MADAME DeCOSTA gave vocal lessons in her studio, located in Dennis Sheedy's old Grant Street mansion. (DPL)

THE *Rocky Mountain News,* a poor second to the *Denver Post* in sensationalism, still was an important Denver daily. (DPL)

150

GREYHOUND MOTOR BUSES took landlocked Coloradoans up over the mountains and as far away as they wanted to go. (DPL)

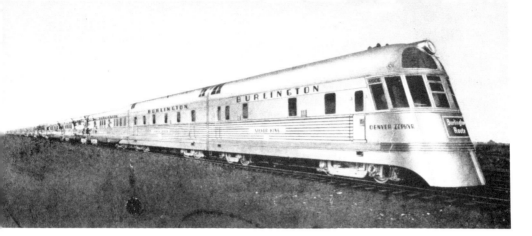

THE DENVER ZEPHYR, "A Symphony in Stainless Steel," boasted "rugged power and velvet speed." The sleek 12-car Zephyrs made the Denver-Chicago run in a mere 16 hours.

LAKESIDE continued to draw its share of bathing beauties—and big-name bands, like Kay Kyser and His Orchestra, which performed in 1937. (DPL)

LOWRY AIR FORCE BASE got underway in 1935 when Denver voters approved a bond issue to purchase the Agnes Phipps Memorial Sanitorium for military use. Two years later, President Roosevelt signed legislation authorizing an initial appropriation of $2.3-million for construction, and late in 1937 the first of 1,500 WPA workers, using wheelbarrows and mules, set to work. (Lowry)

LOWRY'S FIRST TROOPS arrived at Union Station in early 1938. (Lowry)

DWIGHT EISENHOWER posed for this
1938 picture taken by his son. He is sitting
in his mother-in-law's electric. (DPL)

THE PIONEERS in the late 1930s drew thousands of students and fans to the University of Denver stadium. Less than a generation later the school dropped football. (DPL)

GENE FOWLER, once a *Post* reporter, became a successful author with publication of *Timber Line,* the story of Bonfils and Tammen. By 1940, he was a celebrity of sorts, famous for bon mots, such as the one to his friend Lucius Beebe: "Money is something to be thrown off the back end of trains." (DPL)

JITTERBUGGING became as popular as zoot suits and angora sweaters, despite the frowns of its staid critics. (Gates)

155

DENVER DETECTIVES nabbed $1,000 worth of gambling devices in this 1941 raid. Gambling, like whoring, was unpopular mostly with the law. (DPL)

ADVENT OF WORLD WAR II meant gearing up at Lowry Air Force Base. By December 31, 1942, Lowry had 15,860 uniformed personnel and the world's largest barracks. Among the military men was this beaming bomber crew, with Col. Herbert Morgan Jr. (Lowry)

WAC TRAINING was part of Lowry's operations, too. (DPL)

ACTOR GARY COOPER visited wounded airmen at Lowry. (DPL)

THE HOMEFOLKS did their part for the war effort, whether working on the War Production Drive, entertaining troops at the USO, or kissing the boys goodbye. (SHSC-DPL)

BAND LEADER Glenn Miller (shown with his wife) was a favorite at Elitch Gardens before he left for European duty. (DPL)

THE ALLIED INVASION of France brought excitement, hope, and prayer, as did the final attack on Japan in July 1945. (SHSC)

WHEN JAPAN ANNOUNCED its surrender, patriotic Denverites went wild. They walked off their jobs and thronged into the streets, knocking down trolley wires, smashing windows, and stopping traffic downtown. Merchants locked their doors and mothers kept children off the streets, safe from the antics of celebrating servicemen. (DPL)

159